TABLE OF CONTENTS

Executive Summary

In the aftermath of the September 11, 2001, attack there was world-wide sympathy and support for the United States. This was best summed up in the headline in the French newspaper *Le Monde—Nous sommes tous Americains.* ("We are all Americans now.")

Since then, polls conducted by the U.S. Government and respected private firms have revealed a precipitous decline in favorability toward the United States and its foreign policy. The generally positive ratings from the 1950's to 2000 moved to generally negative after 2002. As the very first witness in a 10-hearing series with pollsters and regional analysts told the Subcommittee— *"We have never seen numbers this low."*

The reversal is unprecedented and widespread:

- A 45-percentage point drop in favorability in Indonesia; 41 in Morocco; 40 in Turkey; and 27 in the United Kingdom;

- Among Muslims in Nigeria, favorable opinion fell 33 points, from 71 percent to 38 percent, within an eight-month period;

- A 26-point increase in Europe of the view that U.S. leadership in world affairs is undesirable;

- Unfavorability rose to 82 percent in Arab countries and 86 percent of Latin American elites now rate U.S. relations negatively; and

- 83 percent of countries in 2002 had a plurality of citizens judging the United States favorably; by 2006 only 23 percent of countries had a plurality saying that U.S. influence is positive.

While the United States can't base its foreign policies on opinion polling— either at home or abroad—this consistently negative view of U.S. foreign policy is both a liability and a sign that something has gone seriously awry. What happened? Why, as the question is often posed, do they hate us?

Americans are grasping for the answer and two schools of thought appear to have emerged. One school posits to the average foreigner the motivations attributed to the 9/11 conspirators by President Bush in his address to Congress after the attack:

> *Americans are asking, "Why do they hate us?" They hate what we see right here in this chamber—a democratically-elected government. Their leaders are self-appointed. They hate our freedoms—our freedom of religion, our freedom of speech, our freedom to vote and assemble and disagree with each other.*

Proponents of this school argue that opposition to U.S. leadership among the general public in formerly-colonized countries—and not just among fundamentalist groups like al-Qaeda—is rooted in a "clash of civilizations" between Western and non-Western values. Many also believe that there is a divergence in values between America and the former European Colonial powers themselves—and that this divergence requires the United States to proceed unilaterally.

In sum, this school argues that both radical and general opposition to U.S. leadership are driven by the same motivations: A rejection of American culture, disagreement with American values, and jealousy about American power. For this school, opponents of U.S. leadership are, in a word, anti-American.

The competing school of thought argues that the problem arises not from our culture, values, or power—but rather from our *policies*. This school holds that foreigners perceive as hypocritical the way our policies contradict some of our values and create a variance between our behavior and our rhetoric—for example, when we support non-democratic regimes while we talk about promoting democracy. The perceived hypocrisy, in turn, disappoints foreigners to the point that they oppose cooperation with the U.S. Government. This school rejects the concept of anti-Americanism in favor of a concept of disappointment with our failure to live up to American values.

Adherents of this policy-based school of thought doubt that cultural hatred is the crucial motivation for people who oppose American leadership, whether violently or non-violently. They note that while cultural xenophobia is common to all fundamentalist movements, the major *jihads* in which members of al-Qaeda had participated at the time of 9/11 had been directed against a wide variety of governments. The shared characteristic of these governments was not their national values, but rather that they were seen by the fundamentalists as either oppressing Muslims or supporting regimes that were not, in their opinion, sufficiently Islamic:

- The dictatorial Soviet Union in the 1980's for its invasion of Afghanistan in support of a secular regime;

- Militaristic Serbia in the 1990's for its treatment of Bosnian Muslims;

- Nationalistic Russia for its ongoing domination of Muslim Chechnya; and

- The democratic United States for its military support of repressive regimes in Saudi Arabia and Egypt.

So, which school is right?

* * *

The polling data presented in this report cannot address the beliefs of members of al-Qaeda and similar groups. For the mainstream of foreign citizens, though, the vast weight of polling data provided by our expert witnesses supports the school claiming that disappointment with U.S. policies, rather than anti-Americanism, is the cause of today's record lows in international approval.

Dr. James Zogby, who conducts polls in Muslim countries for Zogby International, expressed this in a nutshell to the Subcommittee: "It's the policies, stupid." Similarly, Dr. Michael Scheuer, the former chief of the CIA's bin Laden unit, noted:

[S]imply look at the polls that have been conducted in the Islamic world over the last 15 years. Inevitably, large majorities in most Muslim countries admire the way Americans live. Inevitably, in an 85–90 percent rate, they hate the impact of our policies in the Islamic world.

The pollsters' testimonies support the conclusion that the decline in international approval of U.S. leadership is caused largely by opposition to the invasion of Iraq, U.S. support for dictators, and practices such as torture and rendition. They testified that this opposition is strengthened by the perception that our decisions are made unilaterally and without constraint by international law or standards—and that our rhetoric about democracy and human rights is hypocritical.

And it is not just Muslim opinion that holds these views. Consider this excerpt from the text that guides Russia's high school teachers of U.S. foreign policy:

> *American foreign policy is designed to dominate the strategic minerals of the Middle East through alliance with dictatorial regimes. In Asia and Latin America, it uses military force to threaten governments who challenge its commercial interests.*

This is the image of America that has come to predominate in much of the world. Accurate or not, this image and the reasons it has spread must be openly discussed and thoughtfully addressed.

The primary finding from the Subcommittee's series of hearings is that the decline in our standing does not appear to be caused by a rejection of such values as democracy, human rights, tolerance, and freedom of speech. Nor is it a reaction to such facets of American life as a high standard of living, mass culture, and economic opportunity, or to the American people—or even to U.S. military power, so long as it is exercised within the framework of international norms and institutions. **All of these were well established and well known prior to 2002 when America's image was at its highest.**

There is, fortunately, a silver lining in this finding. It means that there is something to work with—that there are concrete steps we could take to reverse the dramatic decline in America's reputation. Expressions of disappointment, rather than of hatred, are a call to us to remain true to our values—and an invitation to a frank dialogue, both international and domestic, that is long overdue.

* * *

Another key finding that emerges from the data compiled at our hearings is that substance matters, of course, but style does too. Words do matter. Aggressive rhetoric can have an enormous impact on popular perceptions—particularly if it has been backed up repeatedly by unilateral action. President Bush, Vice President Cheney, and some of their top advisers have twisted President Teddy Roosevelt's wise aphorism into: *Speak loudly and carry a big stick—and show everybody that you're going to use it if they disagree with you.*

Personality, record, and rhetoric have made President Bush deeply unpopular in Latin America, Western Europe, and Muslim countries. In the Muslim world he has achieved the dubious distinction of being more disliked than Israeli leaders, by margins of up to 12–1. The Administration's rhetoric about and unilateral military action against al-Qaeda and Saddam Hussein (and threats against Iran) have been interpreted by the broader Islamic world as creating a paradigm in which conflict is seen as inevitable. Consider the flood of aggressive rhetoric to which Muslims have been exposed by members of the Bush administration or its public proponents:

> *If you're not with us, you're against us ... Bring it on ... Axis of evil ... Islamofascism ... A Crusade ... U.S. soldiers are God's warriors ... The only thing (Arabs) understand is force ... Shock and awe.*

Combine such arrogant rhetoric with the unilateral use of military force, and a refusal to respect international norms on torture and rendition, and the result is the "perfect storm" that has brought down both President Bush's and America's international reputation. In Muslim countries polls found a widespread belief in an American war on Islam and majorities thinking that the United States is a military threat to them. Incredibly, these countries include Turkey, a long-standing U.S. ally, and Kuwait, the country that the United States liberated from Saddam Hussein's rule as part of a United Nations mission in 1991. It is hard to imagine more troubling examples of the decline in America's reputation.

* * *

What Do They Think, and Why? Eight Findings from Polling Data on International Opinion about the United States and its Foreign Policy

The Subcommittee held 10 hearings with a broad range of international policy pollsters and regional analysts. Testimony, transcripts, polling data, and other documents—all of which are available on the Subcommittee's Website—provide concrete information about international opinion based on scientific, large-sample random surveys and on discussions in focus groups.

The Subcommittee identified eight main findings about the levels, trends, and causes of international opinion of American policies, values, and people. These are summarized here and discussed in detail below.

1. *It's true: U.S. approval ratings have fallen to record lows in nearly every region of the world. Generally positive ratings from the 1950's to 2000 have moved to generally negative ratings since 2002. Approval ratings are highest in non-Muslim Africa and lowest in Latin America and in Muslim countries.*

2. *It's the policies: Opposition to specific U.S. policies, rather than to American values or people, has driven this decline.   The key policies are: The invasion and occupation of Iraq; support for repressive governments worldwide; a perceived lack of even-handedness in the Israeli-Palestinian dispute; and torture and abuse of prisoners in violation of treaty obligations.*

3. *It's the perception of hypocrisy: Disappointment and bitterness arise from the perception that the proclaimed American values of democracy, human rights, tolerance, and the rule of law have been selectively ignored by successive administrations when American security or economic considerations are in play.*

4. *It's the unilateralism: A recent pattern of ignoring international consensus, particularly in the application of military power, has led to a great deal of anger and fear of attack. This in turn is transforming disagreement with U.S. policies into a broadening and deepening anti-Americanism, a trend noted by the Government Accountability Office.*

5. *It's the historical memory*: U.S. domination remains a potent image for long periods—and that image is used to discredit current U.S. policies.

6. *It's the lack of contact*: Contact with America and Americans reduces anti-Americanism, but not opposition to specific policies. Visitors to America—particularly students—and even their families and friends, have more positive views about America than non-visitors by 10 percentage points.

7. *It's the visas*: Interaction with the U.S. immigration and the visa process is a significant source of frustration with America. Particularly among Muslim applicants, the experience with customs and border officials creates a perception that they are not welcome. This perception spreads across their communities through their "horror stories" about travel to the United States.

8. *It's the perceived war on Islam*: The combination of all of the previous findings has created a growing belief in the Muslim world that the United States is using the "war on terror" as a cover for its attempts to destroy Islam.

* * *

Finding 1: It's true: *U.S. approval ratings have fallen to record lows in nearly every region of the world. Generally positive ratings from the 1950's to 2000 have moved to generally negative ratings since 2002. Approval ratings are highest in non-Muslim Africa and lowest in Latin America and in Muslim countries.*

In 35 of 42 countries polled by Pew in 2002, ratings for the United States were more favorable than not.[1] Just four years later, in 2006, in 20 of 26 countries polled by the Project on International Policy Attitudes, negative ratings of U.S. influence on the world were higher than positive ones.[2] Putting these two polls together on Chart 1, we can see that 83 percent of countries polled in 2002 had pluralities that were positively inclined toward the United States and its role in the world, compared to only 23 percent in 2006.[3] Some of the reversals in favorability between 1999 and 2006 are dramatic: Comparing State Department and Pew data, there was a 45-point drop in Indonesia, a 41-point drop in Morocco, a 40 point drop in Turkey, and a 27-point drop in the United Kingdom.[4]

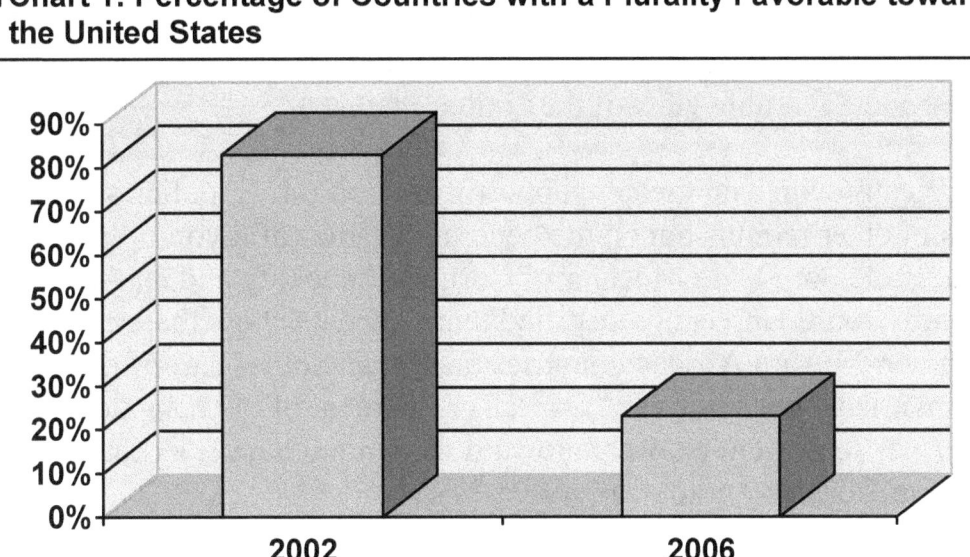

Chart 1: Percentage of Countries with a Plurality Favorable toward the United States

These ratings are at an all-time low:

There has really been no time for which we have data that shows the broad level of dissatisfaction with U.S. foreign policy that we find today [5] *... [This] is definitely unique. We have never seen numbers this low.* "[6] —Dr. Steven Kull, director of the Program on International Policy Attitudes (PIPA) at the University of Maryland.

... certainly over this 25-year period, this is a low point—Dr. Andrew Kohut, president of the Pew Research Center.[7]

A compilation of a wide range of European polls shows that U.S. favorability never dropped below 50 percent in European countries after World War II, even at the height of the Vietnam War under Presidents Johnson and Nixon. This was similarly true in the 1980's under President Reagan, when the United States was engaged in proxy wars in Central America and Africa, and was being harshly criticized in Europe over its policies on nuclear weapons.[8] According to Pew's Andrew Kohut:

President Reagan's tough stand with the Communists was not well received in Europe at the time, but the reaction was not as broad and as deep as it is [today]. [9]

These historical data confirm pollster John Zogby's recollection before the Subcommittee that: *"Ronald Reagan's numbers were very, very good."* [10]

Opposition to U.S. leadership is strongest in the <u>Muslim world</u>: Fewer than one-third of those surveyed in Indonesia, Pakistan, Turkey, Jordan and Lebanon had a favorable view of the United States. [11]

<u>Africans</u> evince no greater support for specific U.S. policies than residents of other regions but on the general question of favorability toward America, Professor Devra Moehler of Cornell University and an Academy Scholar at Harvard University, testified that Pew data show that ratings are higher in non-Muslim African countries than in any other part of the world and are invariably net positive. [12] Overall, 71 percent of the respondents were either very or somewhat favorable toward the United States, by far the highest in the formerly colonized world. [13]

<u>European</u> opposition to U.S. leadership in world affairs as "undesirable" has nearly doubled from 2002 to 2006, from 31 percent to 57 percent. [14] These views show "persistence" according to John Glenn of the German Marshall Fund but "not necessarily a … hardening …" [15] This opposition is particularly troubling, as these countries were long-time allies throughout the Cold War, were ardently supportive of the United States after the 9/11 attack, and many have suffered similar terrorist attacks on their soil.

<u>Latin America's</u> economic and political elites are traditionally more conservative and pro-American than the general public but they currently hold strongly negative views of U.S. policies. In Zogby International's 2006 poll, 86 percent of elites rated U.S. handling of its relations toward Latin America as fair or poor (which the Zogby firm aggregates as negative) and only 13 percent as good or excellent (or positive). [16] Some of the cause may be strongly negative opinion about President Bush personally. According to John Zogby, "At least in a couple of years the President of the United States has gotten lower marks among the elites than Chavez and Castro." [17] Latin Americans as a whole hold a negative view of the American government: 33 percent favorable and 45 percent unfavorable. [18]

<u>Chinese</u> favorability toward the United States is closer to the low ratings of the Middle East than to the mid-range ratings of Europe. Support for the U.S. "war on terror" is at 19 percent in China, similar to the 10

percent in Egypt and the 14 percent in Turkey, but much lower than the ratings in Germany (47 percent), France (43 percent), and Great Britain (49 percent).[19] The only study with comparison across time found that the U.S. "friendship" score of Chinese citizens dropped from 61 percent in 1998 to 39 percent in 2004.[20]

Among many people, rejection of U.S. policies is an intensely-held opinion which makes it difficult to change: 53 percent of people surveyed in the European Union saw the United States as a threat to world peace, roughly the same percentage that saw Iran and North Korea as such a threat.[21] Pew's Andrew Kohut testified that such a level of intensity is a new phenomenon and that by 2005, negative global opinion toward the United States was becoming "entrenched."[22]

Finding 2: It's the policies*: Opposition to specific U.S. policies, rather than to American values or people, has driven this decline. The key policies are The invasion and occupation of Iraq; support for repressive governments worldwide; a perceived lack of even-handedness in the Israeli-Palestinian dispute; and torture and abuse of prisoners in violation of treaty obligations.*

What has driven down international favorability toward the United States and its foreign policy? Some analysts have suggested that the cause is an anti-Americanism based on:

- Jealousy of U.S. military power and economic success;

- A "clash of civilizations" between the West and Islam; and

- A deep "Mars/Venus" cultural division on the use of force, between an activist United States and a pacifist Europe.

The polling data presented to the Subcommittee strongly discount these suggestions and, instead, generally support the consensus among our witnesses that opinion about U.S. policy choices, and not bias or inherent differences between the United States and other countries, have driven the freefall in favorability toward the United States. [23]

Pollster James Zogby said in his summary of the results of large-scale surveys of Arab opinion: "It is the policy, stupid." More formally, he testified that: *"Arabs like our values, they like our people, our culture. In fact, it was our policies they did not like, and this is what drove down our favorable ratings."*[24]

Professors Peter Katzenstein of Cornell and Robert Keohane of Princeton, editors of a recent volume of academic studies on anti-Americanism, report that the percentage of people who call themselves "favorable toward America" is consistently lower than the percentage who judge "life in America" to be superior to life in their own country, with gaps ranging from 11 to 98 percentage points in the 16 countries surveyed.[25] They note that these gaps reflect an interesting message of opposition to U.S. foreign policy and not to America itself: *"Yankee go home ... and take me with you!"*[26] President Bush, among others, has cited this desire to immigrate to the United States as proof that opposition to U.S. leadership is of little strategic importance.[27]

Michael Scheuer, the former chief of the CIA's bin Laden unit, agrees that it is not American values but U.S. policies that have created Muslim opposition:

> *[W]e are at war with militant Islamists, terrorists if you prefer, because of our policies in the Muslim world, not because of what we think or believe.*[28] *... [S]imply look at the polls that have been conducted in the Islamic world over the last 15 years. Inevitably, large majorities in most Muslim countries admire the way Americans live. Inevitably, at an 85–90 percent rate, they hate the impact of our policies in the Islamic world: Unqualified support for Israel ... our support for states who are deemed oppressors of Muslims through the world, especially Russia, China, and India, our present civilian and military [presence] on the Arabian Peninsula, our military presence elsewhere in the Islamic world, and probably, most damagingly, 50 years of support for Arab tyranny.*[29]

According to PIPA's Steven Kull:

> *The problem is not really anti-Americanism. It is not a rejection of what America traditionally has stood for. If anything, it is disappointment that the U.S. is not living up to that image.*[30] *... The unhappiness with the U.S. is not about U.S. values.*[31] *... [Foreign policy is] the aspect of the U.S. that elicits the strongest negative feeling.*[32] *... [Low favorability] cannot be dismissed as something that*

is necessarily engendered by the fact that we are a powerful and rich country. During the 1990's the views were predominantly positive.[33]

Dr. Kull testified that majorities in 66 out of 67 countries agreed that *"democracy may have problems, but it is still better than any other form of government."*[34] He reported further that *"in 19 out of 20 countries polled by Globescan, a majority agreed that 'the free enterprise system is the best system on which to base the future of the world.' "*[35]

According to Pew's Andrew Kohut: *"The problems that we have are not specifically a consequence of differences between values of Americans and values of our allies ... [T]he value gaps don't create the problems, but they exacerbate them ... America was the sole superpower during [the 1990's], and the image of the United States was very positive."*[36]

Cornell professor Moehler agreed: *"[W]ith respect to Muslims within Africa, their attitudes are primarily shaped by United States policies rather than attitudes about U.S. democracy or popular culture ... Primarily Muslims in Africa are more negative because of our policies."*[37]

In a Zogby poll in 2002, it was reported that Arabs consistently have positive views of U.S. values, people, culture and products that exceed their negative views of U.S. policies by as much as 50 to 70 percentage points. For example, Chart 2 shows that the average country percentage of Arabs with favorable views of U.S. freedom and democracy is 54, while the average with favorable views of U.S. policy toward the Arab world is 8, a gap of 46 percentage points.[38]

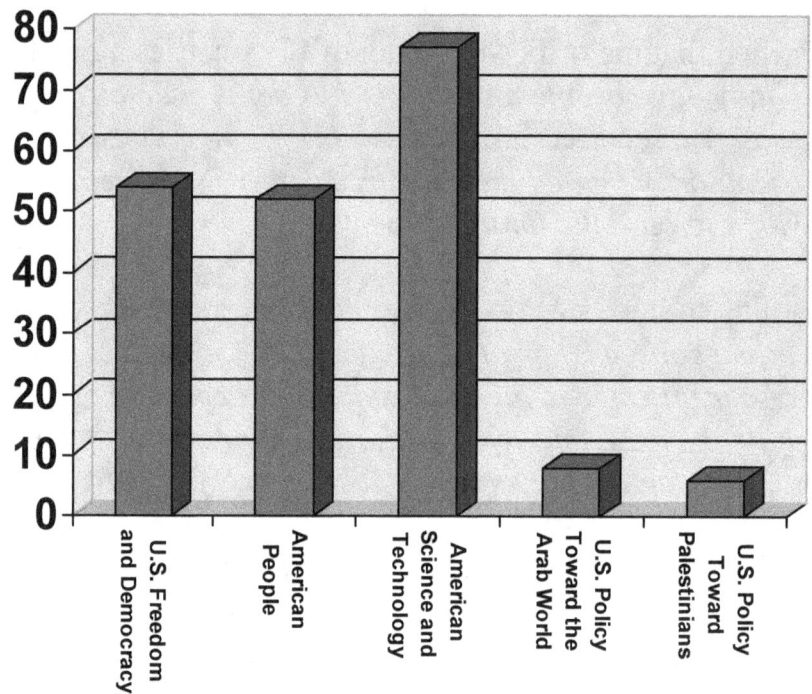

Chart 2: Percentage of Arabs with a Favorable View of the United States

In <u>Europe</u>, according to the German Marshall Fund, Americans and Europeans continue to agree on a wide range of issues and values, from Iran's nuclear program, to phone-tapping, to supporting non-violent democracy promotion abroad.[39] Moreover, contrary to the Mars/Venus hypothesis, Europeans are no more averse to military action than Americans are, provided that the action take place under an international body or agreement: 82 percent of Europeans said they would support military action in a future scenario like the invasion of Iraq if it took place under a UN mandate.[40]

If it is policies and not values that are more at play, then which specific U.S. policies are most responsible for driving support for U.S. leadership down to record lows? The most damaging are described below. It should be noted, though, that the record is not all bad: Good policies can achieve good results in public opinion. For example, U.S humanitarian assistance to Indonesia following the 2004 tsunami improved favorable ratings from 15 percent to 38 percent. However, perhaps reflecting differences in the intensity of opposition to U.S. policy, there was not a similar rise in Pakistan after U.S. earthquake relief in 2005.[41]

Invasion and occupation of Iraq:

- On average, 73 percent of respondents in 26 countries polled by PIPA/GlobeScan disapproved of the U.S. invasion and occupation; [42]

- Among Muslims in Nigeria, favorable opinion toward the United States fell from 71 percent in 2002 to 38 percent within eight months after the invasion of Iraq; [43]

- Andrew Kohut of the Pew Research Center reported that the belief that the war in Iraq has made the world a more dangerous place is in the 60- and 70-percent range for most countries; [44] and

- John Glenn of the German Marshall Fund reported similar results: In 2004, 80 percent of Europeans felt that the invasion and occupation of Iraq was not worth the loss of life and other costs, and 73 percent thought that it had increased the threat of terrorism around the world. [45]

Torture and Rendition: PIPA's Dr. Kull testified that in 1998 the U.S. Information Agency found that an average of 60 percent of people in Germany and the United Kingdom judged the United States to be doing a good job on promoting human rights; by 2007, an average of 67 percent of people in those two countries judged it to be doing a bad job. [46] It is hard for the Subcommittee to escape the conclusion that this reversal is due to the well-publicized reports of "secret prisons" and torture and abuse of prisoners during the intervening years — at Abu Ghraib and Guantanamo prisons, and after "renditions" to countries with a history of torturing prisoners.

An average of 69 percent of people in PIPA/GlobeScan's 26 countries disapprove of U.S. treatment of detainees in Guantanamo and other prisons. [47] Dr. Kull noted that particularly in Europe there had been a rise in disapproval because *"extraordinary renditions are negatively perceived..."* [48] The Center for Strategic and International Studies's Julianne Smith testified that the U.S. image problem in Europe arises from the lack of due process for terror suspects and the violation of human rights during interrogations. [49]

A case involving a Canadian citizen has received a great deal of publicity in both Europe and Canada. Canadian Web consultant Maher Arar was seized during international transit at JFK Airport in New York and rendered to Syria, where he was held at times in a coffin-like cell, and routinely beaten. The Canadian Government, whose erroneous reports led to Arar's inclusion on a U.S. "watch list," has investigated the case, apologized for its error, and made financial compensation. Despite repeated letters from Chairman Delahunt requesting clarification about the "diplomatic assurances" that there would be no torture that were allegedly obtained from Syria, the Bush administration still refuses to provide an explanation of the assurances or of its continuing refusal to permit Arar entry into the United States.

Support for Israel: Pew's Andrew Kohut noted that in the Muslim world, *"the perception of the way that the United States handles the Israeli-Palestinian situation is an 800-pound gorilla"* that is first among the reasons for low U.S. favorability.[50] Dr. James Zogby reported that what 62 percent of Arabs in six countries *"want the United States to do the most is to push for a two-state solution to the Palestinian-Israeli conflict."*[51] He cited a perceived lack of "fairness" in the U.S. position. Dr. Zogby also noted that 65 percent of Arabs disapproved of U.S. support for Israel during its battle with Hezbollah in Lebanon.[52]

Border security: In Latin America, John Zogby interpreted his polling as showing that the elites are similar to Americans on values, but strongly oppose U.S. policies on poverty, trade, Iraq, Guantanamo, Cuba, and immigration.[53] Discussing the intensity of dissatisfaction with the fencing of the U.S. border with Mexico, Mr. Zogby said that to Latin Americans, *"The fence is the moral equivalent of Guantanamo."*[54]

President Bush: Some combination of personality, record, and rhetoric has made President Bush deeply unpopular in Latin America, Western Europe, and Muslim countries:

- In 2007 confidence in Bush's leadership in world affairs stood at 3 percent in Morocco, 5 percent in Argentina, 7 percent in Spain and Pakistan, 8 percent in Egypt, and 14 percent in France, compared to 69 percent in Ghana, 57 percent in Israel, 50 percent in India, 43 percent in the United States, and 36 percent in the Czech Republic.[55]

- He was the most disliked world leader in a poll of six Muslim countries in the Middle East, with margins over Israeli leaders of as much as 3–1 (Saudi Arabia), 6–1 (Egypt) and 12–1 (United Arab Emirates).[56] Negative opinion of him averaged 83 percent in five Western European countries in 2006.[57]

- Among those with an unfavorable view of the United States in 2005, in 11 of 16 countries polled, more people said it was mostly because of George Bush than said it was because of a more general problem with America. In Spain the margin was 5–1; in France and Germany the margin was 2–1.[58] President Bush's re-election made more people unfavorable than favorable to the United States in all of the 15 countries polled —possibly reflecting an anger with Americans for supporting him despite the well-publicized failure to find weapons of mass destruction in Iraq and the revelations of torture at Abu Ghraib.[59]

- His calling Iraq, Iran, and North Korea an "axis of evil" in 2002 was disapproved of by majorities in Britain, France, Germany, and Italy by an average of 63 percent of those polled. Disapproval in the United States was only 34 percent.[60]

Finding 3: It's the perception of hypocrisy*: Disappointment and bitterness arise from the perception that the proclaimed American values of democracy, human rights, tolerance, and the rule of law have been selectively ignored by successive administrations when American security or economic considerations are in play.*

As the previous finding indicated, such values as democracy, human rights, tolerance, and the rule of law are as popular in other regions of the world as they are among Americans. The problem, according Dr. Kull, is that the United States is not perceived as living up to these proclaimed values in the conduct of its foreign policy: *"In the focus groups we have done around the world the complaint we hear again and again is not about U.S. values. It is that the U.S. is hypocritical, that it is not living up to its values."*

Dr. Kull notes, however, that this charge is *"a kind of back-handed compliment, because implicitly what they are saying is that if the U.S. were to live up to its values, that would be something positive."*[61]

Talking democracy and human rights, aiding dictators: In the Middle East's Arab countries, according to Dr. Kull:

Muslims share the world view ... that the U.S. doesn't live up to its ideals of international law and democracy. There have also been some very specific complaints that ... it hypocritically supports non-democratic governments that accommodate U.S. interests.[62]

Writing in Katzenstein and Keohane's volume, Professor Marc Lynch of Williams College judges that opposition to U.S. foreign policy cannot be reduced by traditional "public diplomacy" about shared values, precisely because of this widespread perception that the United States is not using its power to promote its stated values. He cites a Jordanian columnist, Fahd al-Fanik, who writes that: *"It would be a benefit to the entire world and for democracy and freedom if America used its power in the service of these goals."* Lynch finds that even the most strongly negative publics have a genuine hope for such a change. It is sadness, he concludes, and not anger that characterizes opposition to U.S. leadership.[63]

Lynch's detailed content analysis of the al-Jazeera television station shows that even this supposed bastion of anti-Americanism consistently calls on the United States to help, rather than to leave, the Middle East and to live up to its own ideals of fairness and democracy.[64]

The German Marshall Fund found that 71 percent of Europeans support the promotion of democracy in other countries, but Ipsos Public Affairs found that majorities in all the European countries it polled oppose the idea that the United States should promote democracy. The German Marshall Fund's Dr. John Glenn and Kellyanne Conway of the Polling Company agreed in testimony that this disparity occurs because the phrase "democracy promotion" when associated with the United States has for many foreign audiences come to mean a muscular, military-oriented approach that includes invasion and "regime change." [65]

Chinese perceptions: In Katzenstein and Keohane's volume, Harvard Professor Alastair Johnston and Michigan Professor Daniela Stockman report that in addition to a strong suspicion about U.S. hegemony and Bush administration language about "pushing back" or "containing" China over the sensitive subject of Taiwan, two related themes about double standards consistently arise in interviews with Chinese subjects:

- The United States claims the right to interfere anywhere, often violently, while denying this right to other nations; and

- The United States is hypocritical on human rights and democracy, aiding abusive, undemocratic governments that back its economic and military interests, while criticizing China and others for doing the same in Darfur and Zimbabwe.

Johnston and Stockman present an analysis of Chinese media coverage that finds that the phrase "double standard" has become something of a mantra in any treatment of U.S. foreign policy. New stories about U.S. democracy promotion contain the phrase in 64 percent of cases. For mentions of the U.S. war on terror, "double standard" occurs 71 percent of the time, and for U.S. critiques of other countries' human rights records, 69 percent.[66]

Dubai Ports: There is a new complaint in the Middle East about hypocrisy over globalization's central tenet of open trade and investment, which arose from congressional opposition in 2006 to Dubai Ports World operating an American port.[67] According to Dr. James Zogby this was a shock and a "debacle" for Arab opinion of the United States:

> [I]n 2006, number one [complaint], Dubai Ports, which, when we did elite surveys after Dubai Ports, what we were hearing from business people is there is no greater friend in the region than the UAE. This is how you treat your friends?[68]

Nuclear weapons: The U.S. and West European initiative to keep Iran from developing the capacity to produce fuel for nuclear weapons founders in Muslim countries on the charge of hypocrisy. The United States, the United Kingdom, and France all clearly believe that nuclear weapons provide a deterrent against foreign threats to their national interest, and have not fulfilled their pledge under the Non-Proliferation Treaty to negotiate their weapons away in a mutual build-down. Iran's neighbors, who have nuclear weapons, including Pakistan, Israel, Russia, and China, also see their utility. U.S. and European resistance to a treaty for a nuclear-free Middle East, which is clearly aimed at Israel, also bolsters Iran's position.[69]

Finding 4: It's the unilateralism*: A recent pattern of ignoring international consensus, particularly in the application of military power, has led to a great deal of anger and fear of attack. This in turn is transforming disagreement with U.S. policies into a broadening and deepening anti-Americanism, a trend noted by the Government Accountability Office.*

Polling reveals that another element in the decline of America's standing has been U.S. unilateralism. The often-stated belief of American political leaders in our "exceptionalism" appears to grate on international audiences when it is used to justify actions taken without the support, and at times with the opposition of, a strong international consensus.

The data indicate that the United States is opposed by others not because of its global military reach and its economic success but rather because of a unilateral approach to its use of power. These concerns about U.S. unilateralism can be put more bluntly: "It's the process, stupid." Pew's Andrew Kohut testified that of the causes of this perception:

> *"Number one ... is a sense that the United States acts unilaterally, and does not take into account the opinions of other countries ...*[70] *There is a real discomfort with American unilateral power ... [W]e have seen suspicion of that power with regard to our motives ... [M]any of our critics overseas think that we want to rule the world."*[71]

According to PIPA's Steven Kull: *"The theme that comes through repeatedly is that the U.S. does not regard itself as like another country. That the U.S. dictates. That the U.S. imposes ..."*[72] This theme is certainly accentuated by statements of U.S. officials and supporters predicting that Arab opponents will reverse course, and cooperate with U.S. policy after seeing force used.

For example, a U.S. officer in Iraq justified destroying the houses and imprisoning the relatives of suspected attackers by telling the *New York Times*: *"You have to understand the Arab mind. The only thing they understand is force—force, pride and saving face."*[73] Similarly, supporters of the Bush administration calling for the invasion of Iraq popularized the saying that *"the road to Jerusalem goes though Baghdad"*—meaning, in one advocate's words: *"[I]f you change the regime through force in Baghdad, American military power will cast a long diplomatic shadow, and it will be America's decade in the Middle East."*[74]

Dr. Kull notes that U.S. power brings with it a special fear of unilateral action that is not present for other nations: *"[I]f the U.S. is perceived as lowering its standards, even if those standards are still higher than any of these other countries', that is very unnerving to people; because what the U.S. might do in an unconstrained situation could have much more impact than what these other countries could do.*"[75]

Much, but not all, of this fear of U.S. unilateralism appears to arise from cases where the United States is perceived as acting without regard to the United Nations and international agreements. For example, Professor Moehler concludes that: *"As citizens of poor countries, Africans are more likely to believe in the central importance of multilateralism and to oppose foreign policies which systematically undermine the UN."*[76]

Both before it decided to ask the UN Security Council to endorse an invasion of Iraq, and after the Security Council refused to do so, the United States made it abundantly clear that it would not be bound by other nations' opinions on the matter. According to Dr. Kull:

> *[T]he complaint is not really that Saddam Hussein was removed. The complaint is that the U.S. did not get UN approval ... The world is looking for reassurance that the U.S. is constrained by the rules that the U.S. itself has promoted.*[77] *... People are showing more genuine nervousness about again whether the U.S. is ... actually following some new model of its role in the world.*[78] *... There was a majority saying that if the United States got UN approval that would make it all right ... The perception was that the U.S. did not have the right ... to act preemptively relative to Iraq.*[79]

France and Germany had supported with troops or funds the 1991 UN-endorsed war to drive Iraq out of Kuwait, but they did not support the 2003 invasion. However, according to a German Marshall Fund study, 63 percent of French and 50 percent of German subjects said that they would have supported the 2003 invasion had it won a UN mandate.[80] The case of Iran seems to confirm this finding about support for multilateral military action. The German Marshall Fund found that in the context of the multilateral initiative to discourage Iran from developing a capability to build nuclear weapons, nearly as many Europeans (45 percent) as Americans (53 percent) were ready to support taking military action if diplomacy failed.[81]

Analyses in Katzenstein and Keohane's volume reaffirm the polling data. Professor Sophie Meunier of Princeton, in a chapter titled "The Distinctiveness of French Anti-Americanism," attributes French antagonism not to a deep bias but to opposition to unilateral U.S. military action.[82]

Stanford Professor David Kennedy's "Imagining America" notes that: *"We were wealthy and powerful before the invasion of Iraq, but not disliked."* [83] He concludes that there was something about the invasion that produced a profound opposition to U.S. global leadership and a profound suspicion about U.S. motivations. This "something" appears to be unilateralism.

By 2005, after a string of well-publicized speeches and policy documents on unilateralism and the right of U.S. military preemption, such as the new National Security Strategy and the invasion of Iraq, Pew polling found that only 18 percent of the French, 19 percent of the Spanish, and 21 percent of Russians said that the United States takes into account the interests of countries like theirs when making policy. [84]

PIPA's Steven Kull reported that *"in a 14-country poll ... large majorities in 12 of them said that the U.S. is playing the role of world policeman more than it should be. That is a theme that comes through in our focus groups quite a lot."* [85] By using military force without the support of international institutions, the United States creates a fear that Katzenstein and Keohane argue can drive what they call "opinion," meaning disagreement on a policy, into "attitude," or bias against cooperation—and can move "anti-Americanism" from "latent" to "intense." [86]

Among the most shocking data presented to the Subcommittee were polls showing that in many countries, including U.S. allies, majorities believe that a U.S. military attack on their nation is a real possibility. For example, Pew found that 65 percent of people in Turkey, a long-standing U.S. ally, fear that the United States might attack it in a dispute. This belief is replicated in a number of seemingly unlikely countries, where majorities express fears that the U.S. will use force against them, including in Indonesia (80 percent), Pakistan (71 percent), Lebanon, Jordan, Indonesia, Russia, Nigeria, Morocco, and Kuwait. [87]

__Finding 5: It's the historical memory__: U.S. domination remains a potent image for long periods—and that image is used to discredit current U.S. policies.

Polling data and analysis by regional experts confirms that historical memory of U.S. actions in a country can linger for decades, creating the potential for strong negative opinions within its public when current U.S. actions somehow trigger the memory. Katzenstein and Keohane point out that Americans seem to be largely unaware of both the incidents to which foreigners take umbrage and the depth of their anger and suspicion.

According to Dr. Julia Sweig, in her book *Friendly Fire: Losing Friends and Making Enemies in the Anti-American Century*, <u>Latin Americans</u> tend to see today's world against the backdrop of a century of U.S.-supported coups and interventions:[88]

- In <u>Venezuela</u>, U.S. support for the dictator Perez Jimenez in the 1950's (which led to the notorious attack on vice president Nixon in Caracas) remains a common theme in the speeches and publicity of the government of Venezuelan President Hugo Chavez, often as prominent as the more recent U.S. acceptance of the military coup against the democratically-elected Chavez in 2002;

- <u>Chileans</u> can cite details of the campaign of military coups and destabilization that President Nixon and his national security advisor, Henry Kissinger, unleashed on the democratically-elected government of Salvador Allende in the 1970's. The highest negative rating among elites for U.S. relations in Latin America is found in Chile: 95 percent;[89] and

- In fact, nearly every country in Latin America, <u>from Mexico, Guatemala, El Salvador, and Nicaragua in the north to Brazil and Uruguay in the south</u>, can point to a U.S. intervention or support for a cooperative dictator in the past century that had the effect of blocking democracy, permitting gross violations of human rights, and favoring American business and U.S. military interests.

The memory of American domination has the potential to make the Latin American public suspicious of U.S. claims of, for example, occupying Iraq because of concerns for the well-being of Iraqis and their right to a democracy.

Katzenstein and Keohane point out that <u>Spain and Greece</u> have traditionally had the lowest ratings in Europe for "trust" in the United States.[90] It is likely that part of the cause is their histories as post-World War II NATO allies in which the United States backed military dictators.

Iranians live in a virtual state of intellectual siege of imagery of past U.S. policies in the Middle East. The government makes frequent reference to: The 1953 U.S. coup that brought the Shah to power over the democratically-elected Mossadegh government; U.S. arms and training for the Shah's armed forces and internal police; U.S. promotion of the Shah's nuclear program (the very one which today is the subject of such strong U.S. opposition); and U.S. backing for Saddam Hussein in the Iran-Iraq war.

In the Muslim world as a whole, politically-oriented religious figures portray today's U.S. role in the Middle East as a continuation of Western attempts to control the region, starting with the Crusades in 1095 and continuing through British and French colonialism in the 18th through 20th centuries.[91] Osama bin Laden's organization is formally called the "World Islamic Front against Crusaders and Jews." The label of "crusader" is constantly applied to the United States by bin Laden and others in an effort to associate current actions with historical grievances.

Professor Doug McAdam of Stanford University, in a chapter in Katzenstein and Keohane's book titled "Legacies of Anti-Americanism: A Sociological Perspective," attributes some of this type of historical memory to national politicians, who create what he calls "legacy anti-Americanism" with constant references to past U.S. actions. He cites the Philippines, Spain, and Korea as examples.[92]

It is not clear that historical memory crosses borders. Citizens of one country may have negative opinions about U.S. actions in another country, but there is little evidence that they retain them over a long period, as long as those actions do not affect them directly. This suggests, for example, that Abu Ghraib and Guantanamo will fade as issues for European opinion, and may in fact already be doing so, but will last for decades in the Muslim world. However, renditions and secret prisons may have a more lasting impact because they have directly affected both European and Muslim countries.

Historical memory can also work in a positive fashion. According to Dr. Kull, approval of both U.S. leadership and policies is higher in Eastern Europe than in Western Europe, which is a legacy of the U.S. role in the Cold War as the primary opponent of Soviet domination of that region.[93]

Finding 6: It's the lack of contact*: Contact with America and Americans reduces anti-Americanism, but not opposition to specific policies. Visitors to America—particularly students—and even their families and friends, have more positive views about America and Americans than non-visitors by approximately 10 percentage points.*

People gather their information and perceptions about the United States from a wide variety of sources such as domestic and international news media, government portrayal, movies, music videos, and speeches by religious figures. Another important source of information is actual contact with Americans, either in the United States or abroad. Millions of Americans are abroad every year and our Armed Forces alone keep thousands of soldiers, families, and support personnel abroad. In addition, approximately 50 million people come to America each year to visit, work temporarily, or live. All of these categories of people, who meet Americans abroad or here, then pass along their impressions to their friends and family.

Harvard Professor Joseph Nye has suggested that this type of contact drives down negative feelings about the United States.[94] Former Under Secretary of State for Public Diplomacy and Public Affairs Karen Hughes told Chairman Delahunt that foreign student programs in the United States are the best form of public diplomacy. Polling data appear to back up these claims. Pollsters consistently report an approximate 10 percentage point advantage in favorability toward America among those who had either visited the United States or had a friend of relative who had:

- Zogby International found that "Arabs who know Americans, Arabs who visited America … they tend to like our people, our culture, our products and our values more, maybe 10 percent more in every case …"[95] Similarly, Zogby found that people who say "yes" when asked, "Have you been to the United States, would you like to come to the United States, do you have a relative living in the United States … are at times 25–30 points more favorable than those who say no."[96]

- Dr. David Pollock agreed: "[P]eople who have some direct personal experience with Americans, or with the United States, are generally more favorable by a modest but still significant margin."[97]

- Cornell Professor Devra Moehler found that visitors of their relatives were five times more likely to be one category higher in favorability.[98]

- Professor Moehler's analysis of African polling data concluded that: *[A]ttitudes about the U.S. depend less on how much people hear about the U.S. and more on who they hear it from ... [W]e can improve or counter negative attitudes ... by increasing points of personal contact ... [This] would help to ensure that the United States maintains its relatively positive image among the African mass public."* [99]

A particularly powerful form of contact that was mentioned by a number of witnesses is education at American colleges and universities. Moehler states that for U.S. favorability ratings, there would be:

> *"positive benefits we would get from boosting educational opportunity for Africans in the United States, especially because those Africans tend to be ones to become elites in their own countries."* [100]

She notes that for an individual visitor, whether traveler, student, or resident: *"There is a multiplier effect because all of their friends and family, which tends to increase by ... 30 or 40 fold, are also benefiting in terms of their attitudes about the United States ..."* [101]

Increased favorability due to contact, however, does not appear to change people's positions on U.S. policies, such as the invasion of Iraq. Dr. James Zogby reported that among Arabs with favorable attitudes toward America as a result of direct contact, "None of this made them like our policies any better." [102] Similarly, Professor Moehler reported that Africans were 52 percentage points more favorable than unfavorable toward America, but only 18 points more favorable than unfavorable toward U.S. international policies. [103]

Finding 7: It's the visas: *Interaction with the U.S. immigration and the visa process is a significant source of frustration with America. Particularly among Muslim applicants, the experience with customs and border officials creates a perception that they are not welcome. This perception spreads across their communities through their "horror stories" about travel to the United States.*

As noted in the previous finding, visits and educational stays in the United States tend to result in a circle of family and friends hearing, and then holding, more positive views about America. However, the process of trying to gain entry to take part in such activities often has precisely the opposite effect. Particularly since 9/11, travelers report that regulations and U.S. personnel make them feel unwelcome and looked down on, from the start of the application at a U.S. consulate to the end of questioning by the final customs official at the port of entry. Included among these travelers have been a number of high-profile guests, whose treatment is then widely publicized in their countries:

- In 2006 Professor Adam Habib, executive director of the Democracy and Governance program at the premier South African social science institute, the Human Sciences Research Council (HSRC), was detained for seven hours of questioning by the U.S. Government upon his arrival in New York as part of an HSRC delegation meeting with such entities as the Centers for Disease Control, the World Bank, and the Carnegie and Gates Foundations. His visa was then revoked and he was deported. The HSRC protested his treatment and a great deal of South African media attention focused on the case, but the United States never explained its decision. Habib told the media: *"The first time something like this happened to me was during apartheid, in the struggle days. I felt it was highly inappropriate and I feel affronted."*[104]

- As recounted in testimony by Dr. Jerry Melillo, director of the Ecosystems Center at the Marine Biological Laboratory of Woods Hole and also in 2006 the president of the International Council for Science (ICSU), Indian Professor Goverdham Mehta, an organic chemist who is a former director of the prestigious Indian Institute of Science, was denied a visa after extensive questioning at a U.S. consulate in Chenna. He had been invited to lecture at the University of Florida. He told the media: *"It was the most degrading experience of my life."* The ICSU, a global organization that promotes scientific exchange, issued a statement about the denial on behalf of its thousands of scientists from over 100 countries, which included these words: "Nondiscrimination and equity are the essential elements of the principle of universality of science."[105]

- Members of the Russian Duma, meeting with members of the House Foreign Affairs Committee in 2007, reported serious difficulties in their visa and entry process. One of the parliamentarians told

Committee members, *"I like the people here, but I will never come back. I had to go through a very degrading experience to get here."*[106]

The visa process for most visitors includes a healthy fee, a personal interview in a U.S. embassy or consulate, a State Department background check, and then a lengthy, unexplained waiting period as intelligence agencies also run checks. Applicants for business, student, and simple vacation visas may have to return hundreds of miles to the interview site repeatedly. In case after case, business partners or employees of American firms, even those who have previously traveled to the United States, find that they cannot come to meetings in time or at all. The reasons for delays are unexplained and so, to the applicants, are inexplicable.

Zogby polls of Latin America and Muslim countries reveal a common theme: Anger at treatment by the immigration and visa process. These publics believe that U.S. officials are discriminating against them: Latin Americans because of suspicions of illegal immigration and Muslims because of suspicion of terrorist affiliation.

According to Dr. James Zogby, the visa and entry process is perceived as so difficult that: *"These are people who will tell you that they have worked here, lived here, love America, but now are afraid to come into our airports ..."*[107] PIPA's Steven Kull reported that: *"In the focus groups, people very spontaneously brought up these restrictions on immigrations and visas as evidence of ... hostility toward Islam.*[108] *... Almost everybody in the focus groups knew somebody who had had some problem when they came to visit the U.S. or coming to work here or to come and study here."*[109]

The Discover America Partnership, whose executive director, Geoff Freeman, testified before the Subcommittee, commissioned a non-random poll of 2,000 international travelers, primarily from airports in the United Kingdom. Their findings included:

- More than twice as many travelers rated the U.S. entry process as the "world's worst" than gave that rating to any other destination;

- 54 percent of the travelers said that U.S. immigration officials are rude; and

- More of the travelers (70 percent) were more concerned about treatment by U.S. immigration officials than about terrorism or crime in the United States (54 percent).[110]

Mr. Merin recounted an incident in which he personally heard a U.S. immigration official tell a British visitor, "They do not pay me enough to be nice." His question to the Subcommittee was: "How many times will that story be repeated in England, and what impact will it have?"[111]

Finding 8: It's the perceived war on Islam*: The combination of all of the previous findings has created a growing belief in the Muslim world that the United States is using the "war on terror" as a cover for its attempts to destroy Islam.*

The tremendous unpopularity in Muslim countries of the war in Iraq, U.S. treatment of prisoners, and U.S. visa policy have combined with aggressive, unilateralist, and Christian rhetoric that Muslim religious leaders have extracted from statements by prominent Americans to convince a growing number of Muslims that the United States is, in Dr. Kull's words:

> *"trying to weaken and divide Islam ... [and has] entered into a war against Islam itself."*[112]

Recent polls by PIPA found that eight of ten Muslims believed this. Egyptians were most convinced of this (92 percent), followed by Moroccans (78 percent), and Pakistanis and Indonesians (both at 73 percent).[113] Interestingly, all four of these countries have received substantial amounts of U.S. foreign aid, with Egypt being the largest recipient other than Israel over the past 30 years.

The perception of a Christian government inimically opposed to Islam has been promoted by the publicity given in the Middle East to:

- The use of the word "crusade" by President Bush;

- His alleged statements to Palestinian foreign minister Nabil Shaath about his divine inspiration for Middle East policies;

- References to a religious war between Islam and Christianity by a U.S. general and a media commentator; and

- The use of the term "Islamofacism" or the characterization of Islam as a violent and discredited religion by a broad spectrum of American political figures and conservative commentators.[114]

Reports —some accurate, some not—of the denigration of the Koran by U.S. military personnel have also been featured prominently in the Muslim media. On average across three dispersed Muslim countries—Morocco, Pakistan, and Indonesia—64 percent of people think that spreading Christianity to the Middle East is a goal of U.S. policy.[115]

As a result, the phrase, "War on Terror," finds little resonance in the Muslim world:

- In 2006, only 16 percent of Jordanians and 10 percent of Egyptians interviewed by Pew supported the "U.S.-led War on Terror." This contrasts with ratings in the 40's for Britain, France, and Germany;[116]

- According to Pew's Andrew Kohut, *"The war on terrorism is not seen as a legitimate war on terrorism. It is seen as America picking on Muslims, and having other motives…";*[117]

- According to PIPA, this attitude is mirrored in views of the current U.S. administration: 93 percent of Egyptians, 76 percent of Moroccans, 67 percent of Pakistanis, and 66 percent of Indonesians have unfavorable views of the Bush administration;[118]

- Even in relatively friendly sub-Saharan Africa, there is a strong suspicion among the substantial Muslim population about U.S. motives. [119]

The perception of a war on Islam persists despite the fact that its most prominent promoters, al-Qaeda leaders, are not very popular. According to PIPA's Steven Kull, while al-Qaeda's critiques of the U.S. military presence *"resonate with people in the region ... Osama bin Laden is not popular. Now shortly after 9/11 he was sort of a popular figure as somebody who sort of stands up to America, but the more people found out about him, the less they like him, and there is right now no country that has a majority that has a positive view of him."* [120]

In his chapter in Katzenstein and Keohane's book, Professor Marc Lynch agrees with Dr. Kull, arguing that only a minority of Arabs has a bias against the West—and the United States—as an enemy of Islam. [121] He finds that the Arab mainstream remains open to persuasion if controversial U.S. policies are modified.

* * *

Conclusion: America's Monolithic Image

The Subcommittee's series of hearings on the decline in America's reputation revealed that foreign audiences suffer from a number of misconceptions about how the United States makes its decisions on foreign policy. It is often assumed by citizens of other countries that a monolithic American society has lined up behind President Bush's policies on the invasion and occupation of Iraq, Guantanamo, torture, and rendition. American exceptionalism is seen as a national credo rather than a hotly-disputed claim by the Bush administration.

Certainly part of the fault for this misperception lies with the foreign audiences themselves. On its face, it is ill-informed and simplistic to think that an entire nation adopts the positions of its leader. Just as Americans err in equating Venezuela with President Chavez or Iran with President Ahmadinejad, foreigners err in seeing President Bush as the embodiment of America's vision of its role in the world. However, part of the problem is also that executive branch officials and the American media consistently oversimplify the nature of debate and decision-making in U.S. foreign policy.

Too often, the administration's position is portrayed as the unitary American position. Concerned about not projecting a sense of weakness, administration officials make claims about their authorities that are neither reflective of our constitutional tradition nor representative of the reality of our lively debates. They portray dissenting voices—both within and outside the executive branch—as insignificant and irresponsible. Congress is considered, to use Senator Chuck Hagel's comment about the Bush administration deliberations on Iraq, as a "constitutional nuisance and an enemy." Too often, the media report this unitary administration perspective reflexively, lending it credence.

A telling, recent example of this is the administration's attempt to conclude a long-term security agreement with the government of Iraqi Prime Minister Maliki—without the participation of the U.S. Congress. On November 26, 2007, President Bush and Prime Minister Maliki signed a Declaration of Principles to govern the negotiations on the agreement. The Declaration pledged that in the agreement the United States would commit to defending Iraq against both internal and external attack.

The administration informed both the Maliki government and the American media that the proposed agreement would not require congressional approval. Yet repeated hearings in this Subcommittee found expert legal opinion nearly unanimous that the U.S. Constitution requires that security commitments of the type described in the Declaration of Principles be approved by Congress.

After this point had been made in testimony, the administration effectively renounced the security commitments envisioned in the Declaration, but affirmed its intention to include in the agreement the "authority to fight" for U.S. troops. Again, the weight of expert legal testimony held that this would also require congressional approval, but the American media continued to repeat the administration's claim that the proposed U.S.-Iraq agreement was a typical, executive branch, "Status of Forces" agreement. Members of Congress, rather than the media or the executive branch, had to take on the task of informing the Iraqi executive branch and parliament that there was significant dispute within the United States Government about the constitutionality validity of the administration's planned agreement.

Dissent is the trademark of democracy and a strength rather than a weakness that is well worth publicizing. If America's tradition of dissent and dispute on foreign policy could be translated to other societies, and penetrate their public consciousness, the monolithic image that guides foreign perceptions of the United States—and which amplifies many of the problems for America's image that are documented in this report—would become less threatening and more approachable.

While this report concludes that U.S. policy is what matters most of all in creating our international image, it also concludes that rhetoric does matter. The Subcommittee plans to release additional reports—one on the impact of the decline in our image on our national interests and one on recommendations for restoring our reputation. We hope that the administration will take our comments and suggestions in the spirit of partnership in which they are made, and that the media will remind foreign audiences that this sort of interaction is typical of the complex competition of views that creates our democratic foreign policy.

* * *

Endnotes

[1] Katzenstein, Peter J., and Robert O. Keohane, eds. *Anti-Americanisms in World Politics.* Cornell University Press: New York, 2007, pp. 1–2, 15.

[2] *Global Polling Data on Opinion of American Policies, Values and People: Hearing before the Subcommittee on International Organizations, Human Rights, and Oversight of the House Committee on Foreign Affairs,* 110th Cong., March 6, 2007, p. 6.

[3] These two questions can be reasonably compared because polling questions about "the United States" tend to be interpreted by foreigners as questions about U.S. foreign policy, rather than about the quality of life in America. This decline in favorability is consistent with the shift in a smaller sample of 14 countries polled by Pew before and after the invasion of Iraq, of whom 10, or 72 percent, were net favorable before the invasion, but only four, or 29 percent, were net favorable after it. Katzenstein, Peter J., and Robert O. Keohane, eds. *Anti-Americanisms in World Politics.* Cornell University Press: New York, 2007, pp. 1, 15 and 16–17. Zogby data that break down attitudes in the Middle East about various aspects of U.S. policy and American life also support the validity of combining these two questions. *Arab Opinion on American Policies, Values, and People: Hearing before the Subcommittee on International Organizations, Human Rights, and Oversight and the Subcommittee on the Middle East and South Asia of the House Committee on Foreign Affairs,* 110th Cong., 2007, p. 12.

[4] *Global Polling Data on Opinion of American Policies, Values and People: Hearing before the Subcommittee on International Organizations, Human Rights, and Oversight of the House Committee on Foreign Affairs,* 110th Cong., March 6, 2007, p. 7.

[5] *Global Polling Data on Opinion of American Policies, Values and People: Hearing before the Subcommittee on International Organizations, Human Rights, and Oversight of the House Committee on Foreign Affairs,* 110th Cong., March 6, 2007, p. 17.

[6] *Global Polling Data on Opinion of American Policies, Values and People: Hearing before the Subcommittee on International Organizations, Human Rights, and Oversight of the House Committee on Foreign Affairs,* 110th Cong., March 6, 2007, p. 16.

[7] *Global Polling Data on Opinion of American Policies, Values and People: Hearing before the Subcommittee on International Organizations, Human Rights, and Oversight of the House Committee on Foreign Affairs,* 110th Cong., March 14, 2007, p. 23.

[8] Katzenstein, Peter J., and Robert O. Keohane, eds. *Anti-Americanisms in World Politics.* Cornell University Press: New York, 2007, p. 78.

[9] *Global Polling Data on Opinion of American Policies, Values and People: Hearing before the Subcommittee on International Organizations, Human Rights, and Oversight of the House Committee on Foreign Affairs,* 110th Cong., March 14, 2007, p. 17. Statistical analysis shows that concern about the Soviet Union was an important cause of the net positive rating for the United States throughout the Cold War. Katzenstein, Peter J., and Robert O. Keohane, eds. *Anti-Americanisms in World Politics.* Cornell University Press: New York, 2007, p. 88. These data do not appear to be consistent with testimony from Polling Company president Kellyanne Conway, who stated that a *Newsweek* poll in 1983 found that only 25 percent of French people approved of U.S. policies. The Subcommittee searched for that poll but was unable to verify it. *Polling Data on European Opinion of American Policies, Values and People: Hearing before the Subcommittee. on International Organizations, Human Rights, and Oversight and the Subcommittee on Europe of the House Committee on Foreign Affairs,* 110th Cong., 2007, p. 50.

[10] *Polling Data on Latin American Opinion of United States Policies, Values and People: Hearing before the Subcommittee on International Organizations, Human Rights, and Oversight of the House Committee on Foreign Affairs,* 110th Cong., 2007, p. 21. During President Reagan's first term, his favorable ratings exceeded his unfavorable ones in the United Kingdom by 47 to 34 percent, despite a 57 to 28 percent negative rating for his performance. In France during his second term, his favorable ratings exceeded his unfavorable ones by 47 to 18 percent. These polling results make the important point that angry demonstrations, such as those prevalent in both countries, are not necessarily a reliable barometer of overall public opinion. United Kingdom, favorability: MORI poll for the Sunday Times, sample of 1,081, 1984; performance: Gallup poll, sample of 1,000, 1983; France: Sofres poll, sample of 1,000, 1987.

[11] *Global Polling Data on Opinion of American Policies, Values and People: Hearing before the Subcommittee on International Organizations, Human Rights, and Oversight of the House Committee on Foreign Affairs,* 110th Cong., March 14, 2007, p. 9. Zogby International found that in five Arab countries

polled (Saudi Arabia, Egypt, Morocco, Jordan, and Lebanon), unfavorability rose from an average of 71 percent in 2002 to 82 percent in 2006, and that by that year these "negative ratings hardened." See pp. 7, 13.

[12] *African Opinion on U.S. Policies, Values, and People: Hearing before the Subcommittee On International Organizations, Human Rights, and Oversight and the Subcommittee on Africa and Global Health of the House Committee on Foreign Affairs,* 110th Cong., 2007, p. 7. The countries were disproportionately former British colonies, and the sample was disproportionately wealthy, urban, and democratic.

[13] *African Opinion on U.S. Policies, Values, and People: Hearing before the Subcommittee on International Organizations, Human Rights, and Oversight and the Subcommittee on Africa and Global Health of the House Committee on Foreign Affairs,* 110th Cong., 2007, p. 14.

[14] *Polling Data on European Opinion of American Policies, Values and People: Hearing before the Subcommittee on International Organizations, Human Rights, and Oversight of the House Committee on Foreign Affairs,* 110th Cong., 2007, p. 14.

[15] *Polling Data on European Opinion of American Policies, Values and People: Hearing before the Subcommittee on International Organizations, Human Rights, and Oversight of the House Committee on Foreign Affairs,* 110th Cong., 2007, p. 8.

[16] *Polling Data on Latin American Opinion of United States Policies, Values and People: Hearing before the Subcommittee on International Organizations, Human Rights, and Oversight and the Subcommittee on the Western Hemisphere of the House Committee on Foreign Affairs,* 110th Cong., 2007, p. 2.

[17] *Polling Data on Latin American Opinion of United States Policies, Values and People: Hearing before the Subcommittee on International Organizations, Human Rights, and Oversight and the Subcommittee on the Western Hemisphere of the House Committee on Foreign Affairs,* 110th Cong., 2007, p. 32.

[18] *Polling Data on Latin American Opinion of United States Policies, Values and People: Hearing before the Subcommittee on International Organizations, Human Rights, and Oversight and the Subcommittee on the Western Hemisphere of the House Committee on Foreign Affairs,* 110th Cong., 2007, p. 3.

[19] *Global Polling Data on Opinion of American Policies, Values and People: Hearing before the Subcommittee on International Organizations, Human Rights, and Oversight of the House Committee on Foreign Affairs,* 110th Cong., March 14, 2007, p. 11. Similarly, favorable opinion of Americans stands at 46 percent in China, higher than the 36 percent in Egypt and the 17 percent in Turkey, but lower than the ratings in Germany (66 percent), France (65 percent), and Great Britain (69 percent).

[20] Katzenstein, Peter J., and Robert O. Keohane, eds. *Anti-Americanisms in World Politics.* Cornell University Press: New York, 2007, p. 160. They report the perception in China that favorability toward America has declined in recent years, starting perhaps with the bombing of the Chinese embassy in Belgrade in 1999 and continuing with the invasion of Iraq. They found that wealthier, better-educated, better-traveled and informed, and younger are somewhat more positively disposed toward the United States, but that these differences are narrowing.

[21] *Global Polling Data on Opinion of American Policies, Values and People: Hearing before the Subcommittee on International Organizations, Human Rights, and Oversight of the House Committee on Foreign Affairs,* 110th Cong., March 14, 2007, p. 5.

[22] *Global Polling Data on Opinion of American Policies, Values and People: Hearing before the Subcommittee on International Organizations, Human Rights, and Oversight of the House Committee on Foreign Affairs,* 110th Cong., March 14, 2007, pp. 3–4.

[23] Anti-Americanism can be seen as a "bias" against the United States for its characteristics ("who we are") whereas negative opinion can be seen as a judgment about U.S. foreign policy choices ("what we do"). Katzenstein, Peter J., and Robert O. Keohane, eds. *Anti-Americanisms in World Politics.* Cornell University Press: New York, 2007, p. 19 and Table 1.4, p. 22.

[24] *Arab Opinion on American Policies, Values, and People: Hearing before the Subcommittee on International Organizations, Human Rights, and Oversight and the Subcommittee on the Middle East and South Asia of the House Committee on Foreign Affairs,* 110th Cong., 2007, p. 6.

[25] Katzenstein, Peter J., and Robert O. Keohane, eds. *Anti-Americanisms in World Politics.* Cornell University Press: New York, 2007, p. 16.

[26] Katzenstein, Peter J., and Robert O. Keohane, eds. *Anti-Americanisms in World Politics.* Cornell University Press: New York, 2007, p. 16.

[27] "Bush Insists U.S. is Stronger Since He Took Office," by Mort Kondracke, *Roll Call*, February 1, 2008.

[28] *Declining Approval for American Foreign Policy in Muslim Countries: Does It Make It More Difficult to Fight al-Qaeda?: Hearing before the Subcommittee on International Organizations, Human Rights, and Oversight of the House Committee on Foreign Affairs,* 110th Cong., 2007, p. 45.

[29] *Extraordinary Rendition in U.S. Counterterrorism Policy: The Impact of Transatlantic Relations: Hearing before the Subcommittee on International Organizations, Human Rights, and Oversight of the House Committee on Foreign Affairs,* 110th Cong. 2007, p. 32.

[30] *Global Polling Data on Opinion of American Policies, Values and People: Hearing before the Subcommittee on International Organizations, Human Rights, and Oversight of the House Committee on Foreign Affairs,* 110th Cong., March 6, 2007, p. 16.

[31] *Global Polling Data on Opinion of American Policies, Values and People: Hearing before the Subcommittee on International Organizations, Human Rights, and Oversight of the House Committee on Foreign Affairs,* 110th Cong., March 6, 2007, p. 8.

[32] *Global Polling Data on Opinion of American Policies, Values and People: Hearing before the Subcommittee on International Organizations, Human Rights, and Oversight of the House Committee on Foreign Affairs,* 110th Cong., March 6, 2007, p. 7.

[33] *Global Polling Data on Opinion of American Policies, Values and People: Hearing before the Subcommittee on International Organizations, Human Rights, and Oversight of the House Committee on Foreign Affairs,* 110th Cong., March 6, 2007, p. 6.

[34] *Global Polling Data on Opinion of American Policies, Values and People: Hearing before the Subcommittee on International Organizations, Human Rights, and Oversight of the House Committee on Foreign Affairs,* 110th Cong., March 6, 2007, p. 14.

[35] *Global Polling Data on Opinion of American Policies, Values and People: Hearing before the Subcommittee on International Organizations, Human Rights, and Oversight of the House Committee on Foreign Affairs,* 110th Cong., March 6, 2007, p. 14.

[36] *Global Polling Data on Opinion of American Policies, Values and People: Hearing before the Subcommittee on International Organizations, Human Rights, and Oversight of the House Committee on Foreign Affairs,* 110th Cong., March 14, 2007, p. 6.

[37] *African Opinion on U.S. Policies, Values, and People: Hearing before the Subcommittee On International Organizations, Human Rights, and Oversight and the Subcommittee on Africa and Global Health of the House Committee on Foreign Affairs,* 110th Cong., 2007, p. 11.

[38] *Arab Opinion on American Policies, Values, and People: Hearing before the Subcommittee on International Organizations, Human Rights, and Oversight and the Subcommittee on the Middle East and South Asia of the House Committee on Foreign Affairs,* 110th Cong., 2007, p. 12. Arabs are clearly aware of the distinction between values and policies: 81 percent of those polled by Zogby International said that U.S. policies are more determinative of their attitude toward us than U.S. values. These findings are generally confirmed in academic studies of opinion, in Katzenstein, Peter J., and Robert O. Keohane, eds. Anti-Americanisms in World Politics. Cornell University Press: New York, 2007, pp. 33, 197-198, 316.

[39] *Polling Data on European Opinion of American Policies, Values and People: Hearing before the Subcommittee on International Organizations, Human Rights, and Oversight and the Subcommittee on Europe of the House Committee on Foreign Affairs,* 110th Cong., 2007. Majorities agree that Iran poses an increasing threat to global security (73 percent of Americans, 58 percent of Europeans); majorities oppose greater governmental authority to monitor citizens' telephone calls as part of the effort to prevent terrorism (58 percent for both Americans and Europeans); and both populations strongly support non-violent democracy promotion abroad, such as monitoring elections (79 percent of Europeans and 67 percent of Americans) and aiding independent organizations such as trade unions and human rights groups (77 percent of Europeans and 71 percent of Americans).

[40] *Polling Data on European Opinion of American Policies, Values and People: Hearing before the Subcommittee on International Organizations, Human Rights, and Oversight and the Subcommittee on Europe of the House Committee on Foreign Affairs,* 110th Cong., 2007, p. 69, p. 20. However, this finding appears to contradict the polling result that 62 percent of Europeans, compared to 20 percent of Americans, say that war is never necessary to obtain justice.

[41] *Global Polling Data on Opinion of American Policies, Values and People: Hearing before the Subcommittee on International Organizations, Human Rights, and Oversight of the House Committee on Foreign Affairs,* 110th Cong., March 14, 2007, p. 7.

[42] *Global Polling Data on Opinion of American Policies, Values and People: Hearing before the Subcommittee on International Organizations, Human Rights, and Oversight of the House Committee on Foreign Affairs,* 110th Cong., March 6, 2007, p. 7.

[43] *Global Polling Data on Opinion of American Policies, Values and People: Hearing before the Subcommittee on International Organizations, Human Rights, and Oversight of the House Committee on Foreign Affairs,* 110th Cong., March 14, 2007, p. 4.

[44] For example, 76 percent of the French, 74 percent of Jordanians, 70 percent of Turks, 70 percent of Egyptians, 68 percent of Spaniards, 66 percent of Germans, and 61 percent of Japanese. *Global Polling Data on Opinion of American Policies, Values and People: Hearing before the Subcommittee on International Organizations, Human Rights, and Oversight of the House Committee on Foreign Affairs,* 110th Cong., March 14, 2007, p. 12.

[45] *Polling Data on European Opinion of American Policies, Values and People: Hearing before the Subcommittee on International Organizations, Human Rights, and Oversight and the Subcommittee on Europe of the House Committee on Foreign Affairs,* 110th Cong., 2007, p. 9.

[46] *Global Polling Data on Opinion of American Policies, Values and People: Hearing before the Subcommittee on International Organizations, Human Rights, and Oversight of the House Committee on Foreign Affairs,* 110th Cong., March 6, 2007, p. 8.

[47] *Global Polling Data on Opinion of American Policies, Values and People: Hearing before the Subcommittee on International Organizations, Human Rights, and Oversight of the House Committee on Foreign Affairs,* 110th Cong., March 6, 2007, p. 7.

[48] *Global Polling Data on Opinion of American Policies, Values and People: Hearing before the Subcommittee on International Organizations, Human Rights, and Oversight of the House Committee on Foreign Affairs,* 110th Cong., March 6, 2007 p. 26.

[49] *Extraordinary Rendition in U.S. Counterterrorism Policy: The Impact of Transatlantic Relations: Hearing before the Subcommittee on International Organizations, Human Rights, and Oversight of the House Committee on Foreign Affairs,* 110th Cong. 2007. A European Parliament investigation on renditions, which was the subject of a Subcommittee briefing prior to one of the hearings in this series, has confirmed reported U.S. policies on renditions and secret prisons.

[50] *Global Polling Data on Opinion of American Policies, Values and People: Hearing before the Subcommittee on International Organizations, Human Rights, and Oversight of the House Committee on Foreign Affairs,* 110th Cong., March 14, 2007, p. 5.

[51] *Arab Opinion on American Policies, Values, and People: Hearing before the Subcommittee on International Organizations, Human Rights, and Oversight and the Subcommittee on the Middle East and South Asia of the House Committee on Foreign Affairs,* 110th Cong., 2007, p. 36.

[52] *Arab Opinion on American Policies, Values, and People: Hearing before the Subcommittee on International Organizations, Human Rights, and Oversight and the Subcommittee on the Middle East and South Asia of the House Committee on Foreign Affairs,* 110th Cong., 2007.

[53] *Polling Data on Latin American Opinion of United States Policies, Values and People: Hearing before the Subcommittee on International Organizations, Human Rights, and Oversight and the Subcommittee on the Western Hemisphere of the House Committee on Foreign Affairs,* 110th Cong., 2007, p. 3.

[54] *Polling Data on Latin American Opinion of United States Policies, Values and People: Hearing before the Subcommittee on International Organizations, Human Rights, and Oversight and the Subcommittee on the Western Hemisphere of the House Committee on Foreign Affairs,* 110th Cong., 2007, p. 24.

[55] Pew Global Attitudes Project, May 2007. Question 56a.

[56] Zogby/Sadar Chari Poll of Arab Countries, February 2007.

[57] Harris Interactive/France 24/Le Monde Poll, December 2006.

[58] Pew Global Attitudes Project, May 2005, Q7, Q10. These low ratings were achieved despite a public relations campaign in early 2005 that included a high-profile visit to Europe by President Bush and Secretary of State Rice.

[59] Pew Global Attitudes Project, May 2005, Q7, Q10.

[60] Pew Research Center poll, April 2002, Q2b.

[61] *Global Polling Data on Opinion of American Policies, Values and People: Hearing before the Subcommittee on International Organizations, Human Rights, and Oversight of the House Committee on Foreign Affairs,* 110th Cong., March 6, 2007, p. 8.

[62] *Declining Approval for American Foreign Policy in Muslim Countries: Does It Make It More Difficult to Fight al-Qaeda?: Hearing before the Subcommittee on International Organizations, Human Rights, and Oversight of the House Committee on Foreign Affairs,* 110th Cong., 2007, p. 5.

[63] Katzenstein, Peter J., and Robert O. Keohane, eds. *Anti-Americanisms in World Politics.* Cornell University Press: New York, 2007, p. 203.

[64] Katzenstein, Peter J., and Robert O. Keohane, eds. *Anti-Americanisms in World Politics.* Cornell University Press: New York, 2007, p. 218.

[65] *Polling Data on European Opinion of American Policies, Values and People: Hearing before the Subcommittee on International Organizations, Human Rights, and Oversight and the Subcommittee on Europe of the House Committee on Foreign Affairs,* 110th Cong., 2007, p. 68, 70, 72, 73. In an analysis in Katzenstein and Keohane that is consistent with these data, Lynch argues that there is some evidence that the use of the word "democracy" by U.S. officials triggers opposition to proposed reforms. This occurs, according to Lynch, not because of a rejection of democracy, but because this use by the United States is associated historically with domination, interference, or invasion.   In this sense, the United States is giving "democracy" a bad name, according to Lynch. Katzenstein, Peter J., and Robert O. Keohane, eds. *Anti-Americanisms in World Politics.* Cornell University Press: New York, 2007, pp. 199, 216.

[66] Katzenstein, Peter J., and Robert O. Keohane, eds. *Anti-Americanisms in World Politics.* Cornell University Press: New York, 2007, p. 161.

[67] *Arab Opinion on American Policies, Values, and People: Hearing before the Subcommittee on International Organizations, Human Rights, and Oversight and the Subcommittee on the Middle East and South Asia of the House Committee on Foreign Affairs,* 110th Cong., 2007, pp. 7, 31.

[68] *Arab Opinion on American Policies, Values, and People: Hearing before the Subcommittee on International Organizations, Human Rights, and Oversight and the Subcommittee on the Middle East and South Asia of the House Committee on Foreign Affairs,* 110th Cong., 2007, p. 31.

[69] See the website of Proliferation Press, posting of October 18, 2007, "Egypt Protests Eroding EU Support for Middle East Nuclear Free Zone." http://proliferationpress.wordpress.com/2007/10/18/egypt-protests-eroding-eu-support-for-middle-east-nuclear-free-zone/

[70] *Global Polling Data on Opinion of American Policies, Values and People: Hearing before the Subcommittee on International Organizations, Human Rights, and Oversight of the House Committee on Foreign Affairs,* 110th Cong., March 14, 2007, p. 5.

[71] *Global Polling Data on Opinion of American Policies, Values and People: Hearing before the Subcommittee on International Organizations, Human Rights, and Oversight of the House Committee on Foreign Affairs,* 110th Cong., March 14, 2007, p. 6.

[72] *Global Polling Data on Opinion of American Policies, Values and People: Hearing before the Subcommittee on International Organizations, Human Rights, and Oversight of the House Committee on Foreign Affairs,* 110th Cong., March 6, 2007, p. 23.

[73] The U.S. officer was Army Captain Todd Brown, quoted in *The New York Times*, in "A Region Inflamed," by Dexter Filkins, December 7, 2003.

[74] For example, Professor Robert Lieber of Georgetown University's Department of Government, speaking at a "Table Talk" event at American University, November 14, 2002. The quotation comes from Washington Institute Visiting Fellow Raymond Tanter (http://truthnews.com/world/2002063343.htm).

[75] *Declining Approval for American Foreign Policy in Muslim Countries: Does It Make It More Difficult to Fight al-Qaeda?: Hearing before the Subcommittee on International Organizations, Human Rights, and Oversight of the House Committee on Foreign Affairs,* 110th Cong., 2007, p. 54.

[76] *African Opinion on U.S. Policies, Values, and People: Hearing before the Subcommittee on International Organizations, Human Rights, and Oversight and the Subcommittee on Africa and Global Health of the House Committee on Foreign Affairs,* 110th Cong. 2007, p. 12. It should be noted that support for multilateralism does not necessarily mean support for the United Nations. As Dr. Pollock noted in testimony, disappointment with the UN's inability to promote peace settlements has led to majorities in Egypt and Jordan holding negative opinions of the UN.

[77] *Global Polling Data on Opinion of American Policies, Values and People: Hearing before the Subcommittee on International Organizations, Human Rights, and Oversight of the House Committee on Foreign Affairs,* 110th Cong., March 6, 2007, p. 9.

[78] *Global Polling Data on Opinion of American Policies, Values and People: Hearing before the Subcommittee on International Organizations, Human Rights, and Oversight of the House Committee on Foreign Affairs,* 110th Cong., March 6, 2007, p. 19.

[79] *Global Polling Data on Opinion of American Policies, Values and People: Hearing before the Subcommittee on International Organizations, Human Rights, and Oversight of the House Committee on Foreign Affairs,* 110th Cong., March 6, 2007, p. 25.

[80] *Polling Data on European Opinion of American Policies, Values and People: Hearing before the Subcommittee on International Organizations, Human Rights, and Oversight and the Subcommittee on Europe of the House Committee on Foreign Affairs,* 110th Cong., 2007, p. 68.

[81] *Polling Data on European Opinion of American Policies, Values and People: Hearing before the Subcommittee on International Organizations, Human Rights, and Oversight and the Subcommittee on Europe of the House Committee on Foreign Affairs,* 110th Cong., 2007, p. 33.

[82] Katzenstein, Peter J., and Robert O. Keohane, eds. *Anti-Americanisms in World Politics.* Cornell University Press: New York, 2007, p. 130.

[83] Katzenstein, Peter J., and Robert O. Keohane, eds. *Anti-Americanisms in World Politics.* Cornell University Press: New York, 2007, Chapter 2.

[84] *Global Polling Data on Opinion of American Policies, Values and People: Hearing before the Subcommittee on International Organizations, Human Rights, and Oversight of the House Committee on Foreign Affairs,* 110th Cong., March 14, 2007, p. 12.

[85] *Global Polling Data on Opinion of American Policies, Values and People: Hearing before the Subcommittee on International Organizations, Human Rights, and Oversight of the House Committee on Foreign Affairs,* 110th Cong., March 6, 2007, p. 7.

[86] Katzenstein, Peter J., and Robert O. Keohane, eds. *Anti-Americanisms in World Politics.* Cornell University Press: New York, 2007, pp. 10-11, 34-35. See also p. 311, which refers to Table 1.7, p. 29.

[87] *Global Polling Data on Opinion of American Policies, Values and People: Hearing before the Subcommittee on International Organizations, Human Rights, and Oversight of the House Committee on Foreign Affairs,* 110th Cong., March 14, 2007, p. 9, and March 6, 2007, p. 15.

[88] See Chapter One, "Cold War History and the Latin American Laboratory," Public Affairs Books, New York, 2007.

[89] *Polling Data on Latin American Opinion of United States Policies, Values and People: Hearing before the Subcommittee on International Organizations, Human Rights, and Oversight and Subcommittee on the Western Hemisphere of the House Committee on Foreign Affairs,* 110th Cong., 2007, p. 3.

[90] Katzenstein, Peter J., and Robert O. Keohane, eds. *Anti-Americanisms in World Politics.* Cornell University Press: New York, 2007, Page 18.

[91] Lawrence, Bruce. *Messages to the World: The Statements of Osama bin Laden.* London: Verso, 2005, p 7.

[92] Katzenstein, Peter J., and Robert O. Keohane, eds. *Anti-Americanisms in World Politics.* Cornell University Press: New York, 2007, Chapter 9.

[93] *Global Polling Data on Opinion of American Policies, Values and People: Hearing before the Subcommittee on International Organizations, Human Rights, and Oversight of the House Committee on Foreign Affairs,* 110th Cong., March 6, 2007, p. 19. Similarly, older Africans lionize Cuba today because of a series of interventions more than 20 years ago in which, as recounted by Johns Hopkins professor Piero Glejesies in *Conflicting Missions: Havana, Washington, and Africa, 1959-1976* (University of North Carolina Press, Chapel Hill, 2003), it shipped aid to the Algerian independence struggle in 1961, supported Che Guevara's military mission to assist Lumumbists in Congo in 1964, and finally used its own regular Army and Air Force to defeat the U.S.-backed South African invasions of Angola in 1975 and 1987. South Africa's government, in particular, which is a major force in continent-wide initiatives like the African Union, continues to respond favorably to governments, such as Libya, Sweden, Russia, and Cuba, and movements, such as the Polisario, who supported its liberation struggle decades ago.

[94] Joseph S. Nye, *Soft Power: The Meaning of Success in World Politics*, Perseus Books Group, New York, 2004.

[95] *Arab Opinion on American Policies, Values, and People: Hearing before the Subcommittee on International Organizations, Human Rights, and Oversight and the Subcommittee on the Middle East and South Asia of the House Committee on Foreign Affairs,* 110th Cong., 2007, p. 7.

[96] *Polling Data on Latin American Opinion of United States Policies, Values and People: Hearing before the Subcommittee on International Organizations, Human Rights, and Oversight and the Subcommittee on the Western Hemisphere of the House Committee on Foreign Affairs,* 110th Cong., 2007, p. 28.

[97] *Arab Opinion on American Policies, Values, and People: Hearing before the Subcommittee on International Organizations, Human Rights, and Oversight and the Subcommittee on the Middle East and South Asia of the House Committee on Foreign Affairs,* 110th Cong., 2007, p. 53.

[98] A statistical analysis by Professor Moehler isolated the characteristics of Africans favoring the United States, and found that the link between contact and favorability was a causal one, and not an artifact of people who were more favorable toward the United States seeking out opportunities to interact with Americans. According to Professor Moehler, after removing this artifact mathematically, "information from friends and relatives in the U.S. has a very positive effect, as does personal experiences of travel to the United States." *African Opinion on U.S. Policies, Values, and People: Hearing before the Subcommittee on International Organizations, Human Rights, and Oversight and the Subcommittee on Africa and Global Health of the House Committee on Foreign Affairs,* 110th Cong., 2007, p. 9, 18.

[99] *African Opinion on U.S. Policies, Values, and People: Hearing before the Subcommittee on International Organizations, Human Rights, and Oversight and the Subcommittee on Africa and Global Health of the House Committee on Foreign Affairs,* 110th Cong., 2007, p. 6-7, 12.

[100] *African Opinion on U.S. Policies, Values, and People: Hearing before the Subcommittee on International Organizations, Human Rights, and Oversight and the Subcommittee on Africa and Global Health of the House Committee on Foreign Affairs,* 110th Cong., 2007, p. 46.

[101] *African Opinion on U.S. Policies, Values, and People: Hearing before the Subcommittee on International Organizations, Human Rights, and Oversight and the Subcommittee on Africa and Global Health of the House Committee on Foreign Affairs,* 110th Cong., 2007, p. 41.

[102] *Arab Opinion on American Policies, Values, and People: Hearing before the Subcommittee on International Organizations, Human Rights, and Oversight and Subcommittee on the Middle East and South Asia of the House Committee on Foreign Affairs,* 110th Cong., 2007, p. 7.

[103] *African Opinion on U.S. Policies, Values, and People: Hearing before the Subcommittee on International Organizations, Human Rights, and Oversight and Subcommittee on Africa and Global Health of the House Committee on Foreign Affairs,* 110th Cong., 2007, p. 16.

[104] "Row Brews as HSRC Demands Answers from US," *Cape Argus,* Cape Town, October 25, 2006.

[105] *International Students and Visiting Scholars: Trends, Barriers, and Implications for American Universities and U.S. Foreign Policy: Hearing before the Subcommittee on International Organizations, Human Rights, and Oversight of the House Committee on Foreign Affairs, and the Subcommittee on Higher Education, Lifelong Learning and Competitiveness of the House Committee on Education and Labor,* 110th Cong., 2007, p. 87.

[106] *International Students and Visiting Scholars: Trends, Barriers, and Implications for American Universities and U.S. Foreign Policy: Hearing before the Subcommittee on International Organizations, Human Rights, and Oversight of the House Committee on Foreign Affairs, and the Subcommittee on Higher Education, Lifelong Learning and Competitiveness of the House Committee on Education and Labor,* 110th Cong., 2007, p. 93.

[107] *Arab Opinion on American Policies, Values, and People: Hearing before the Subcommittee on International Organizations, Human Rights, and Oversight and the Subcommittee on the Middle East and South Asia of the House Committee on Foreign Affairs,* 110th Cong., 2007, p. 37.

[108] *Declining Approval for American Foreign Policy in Muslim Countries: Does It Make It More Difficult to Fight al-Qaeda?: Hearing before the Subcommittee on International Organizations, Human Rights, and Oversight of the House Committee on Foreign Affairs,* 110th Cong., 2007, p. 9.

[109] *Declining Approval for American Foreign Policy in Muslim Countries: Does It Make It More Difficult to Fight al-Qaeda?: Hearing before the Subcommittee on International Organizations, Human Rights, and Oversight of the House Committee on Foreign Affairs,* 110th Cong., 2007, p. 50.

[110] *Welcome to America?: Hearing before the Subcommittee on International Organizations, Human Rights, and Oversight of the House Committee on Foreign Affairs,* 110th Cong., 2007, p. 25.

[111] *Welcome to America?: Hearing before the Subcommittee on International Organizations, Human Rights, and Oversight of the House Committee on Foreign Affairs,* 110th Cong., 2007, p. 37.

[112] *Global Polling Data on Opinion of American Policies, Values and People: Hearing before the Subcommittee on International Organizations, Human Rights, and Oversight of the House Committee on Foreign Affairs,* 110th Cong., March 6, 2007 p. 25, and *Declining Approval for American Foreign Policy in Muslim Countries: Does It Make It More Difficult to Fight al-Qaeda?: Hearing before the Subcommittee on International Organizations, Human Rights, and Oversight of the House Committee on Foreign Affairs,* 110th Cong., 2007, p. 5.

[113] *Declining Approval for American Foreign Policy in Muslim Countries: Does It Make It More Difficult to Fight al-Qaeda?: Hearing before the Subcommittee on International Organizations, Human Rights, and Oversight of the House Committee on Foreign Affairs,* 110th Cong., 2007, p. 11.

[114] According to *The Guardian* of November 7, 2005, Shaath claimed: "President Bush said to all of us: 'I am driven with a mission from God'. God would tell me, 'George go and fight these terrorists in Afghanistan'. And I did. And then God would tell me 'George, go and end the tyranny in Iraq'. And I did … and now, again, I feel God's words coming to me, 'Go get the Palestinians their state and get the Israelis their security, and get peace in the Middle East'. And, by God, I'm gonna do it." The U.S. general was Army Lt. Gen. William Boykin. According to *The International Herald Tribune* of October 20, 2003, Boykin linked Islamic enemies to "Satan" and called U.S. troops "God's warriors" and a Somali military leader an "idol-worshipper." The media commentator was Ann Coulter, who wrote in a 2001 column, "We should invade their countries, kill their leaders and convert them to Christianity." "Islamofacism" is a term used by think-tanks such as the Committee on the Present Danger and the Center for Security Policy, and by commentators such as Norman Podhoretz, and former Senator Rick Santorum.

[115] *Declining Approval for American Foreign Policy in Muslim Countries: Does It Make It More Difficult to Fight al-Qaeda?: Hearing before the Subcommittee on International Organizations, Human Rights, and Oversight of the House Committee on Foreign Affairs,* 110th Cong., 2007, p. 22. The question was not permitted by the Egyptian government.

[116] *Global Polling Data on Opinion of American Policies, Values and People: Hearing before the Subcommittee on International Organizations, Human Rights, and Oversight of the House Committee on Foreign Affairs,* 110th Cong., March 14, 2007, p. 11.

[117] *Global Polling Data on Opinion of American Policies, Values and People: Hearing before the Subcommittee on International Organizations, Human Rights, and Oversight of the House Committee on Foreign Affairs,* 110th Cong., March 14, 2007, p. 5.

[118] "Muslim Public Opinion on US Policy, Attacks on Civilians and al-Qaeda," WorldPublicOpinion.org, April 24, 2007, questions Q24-F25a.

[119] *African Opinion on U.S. Policies, Values, and People: Hearing before the Subcommittee on International Organizations, Human Rights, and Oversight and the Subcommittee on Africa and Global Health of the House Committee on Foreign Affairs,* 110th Cong. (2007), p. 18. Professor Moehler's analysis of individual Africans found that the strongest predictor of unfavorability toward the United States was being Muslim. This standardized effect of someone being 27 times more likely to be one category more unfavorable toward the United States was three times as powerful as the next strongest results, which was that people were nine times more likely to be one category more favorable toward the United States if they were Catholic. Pew's Andrew Kohut reported that largely-Muslim Northern Nigeria is closer to Arab countries than sub-Saharan counties in its disapproval rates. *Global Polling Data on Opinion of American Policies, Values and People: Hearing before the Subcommittee on International Organizations, Human Rights, and Oversight of the House Committee on Foreign Affairs,* 110th Cong., March 14, 2007.

[120] *Global Polling Data on Opinion of American Policies, Values and People: Hearing before the Subcommittee on International Organizations, Human Rights, and Oversight of the House Committee on Foreign Affairs,* 110th Cong., March 6, 2007, p. 24.

[121] Katzenstein, Peter J., and Robert O. Keohane, eds. *Anti-Americanisms in World Politics.* Cornell University Press: New York, 2007, p. 209.

Comments on

"The Decline of America's Reputation: Why?"

"While I respect the idea that public opinion is important, what is most important is to do what is right in building a future." (Statement at the House Foreign Affairs Committee on March 22, 2007).

—SUBCOMMITTEE RANKING MEMBER DANA ROHRABACHER

Following the election of President George W. Bush, many Democratic Members of Congress undermined the War on Terror by attempting to tarnish it as being something other than a genuine struggle to protect our citizens and to bring stability to the Middle East through the establishment of democratic forms of government. For purely domestic political considerations, a tremendous amount of disinformation has been generated which in turn has had a deleterious effect overseas on the image of the United States.

The President of the United States is a strong supporter of the State of Israel. That support does not sit well with most Muslim nations. The President of the United States claims to be a strong supporter of democratic forms of government. That claim threatens some despotic regimes in the Middle East. The effort by the current majority in Congress to depict our nation's effort in the region as being something than a noble one has found a ripe and fertile ground. The separation between fact and fantasy is slim in most of the Middle East due to the fact that media content and educational material are controlled by authoritarian religious governments.

In addition to U.S. domestic contribution to the declining image of the United States, a great deal of animosity results from having to encourage or even persuade people to do what they otherwise would not want to do, to foster the emergence of democratic systems of government around the world. During periods of change, leaders often incur negative ratings as a result of challenging the status quo.

Prior to his last 6 months as president, the most hated politician in American history, Abraham Lincoln, challenged the status quo, stood for morality, and lead America in a new direction—and for that his ratings plummeted. In order to correct the moral backwardness of his time, Abraham Lincoln led the United States through the nation's greatest crisis, the Civil War, during which time he received critical public opinion ratings. However, as a result, the United States began a transition toward moral correctness. Today, the Lincoln Memorial resonates as a beacon of the responsibility of the United States to spread freedom and liberty.

Ronald Reagan was another American President to persevere in the face of low popularity. His ratings dipped significantly when he decided to actively campaign against communism, instead of attempting to wait it out.

During his presidency, Reagan's ratings dropped in Western Europe, even in Berlin. When the Berlin wall came down in 1989, his numbers rebounded in the same fashion as Abraham Lincoln's—according to Steven Kull, "Nothing succeeds like success." (Testimony to the House Foreign Affairs Committee on March 6, 2007.) And success may be the key to rebounding the current number as well. The United States retains international prestige for the ideals such as freedom and democracy that it stands for in the Middle East and must protect in order to reaffirm its commitment to these principles.

In addition to uneasiness over challenging the status quo, the effect of centrally controlled media also influences the perception of the United States. Although the Internet offers many countries more information, not all countries benefit from the freedom of the information age. The United States cannot compete in public opinion polls against nations, and even non-state actors and terrorists that hinder their citizen's ability to access current and accurate information. Propaganda campaigns against the United States considerably reduce its international image.

The war on terror threatens U.S. national security in historically unprecedented ways resulting in stricter visa controls and regulation, which foreigners may seem aggressive and unwelcoming. While no one could disagree with developing more efficient visa control, simply loosening visa control and adding additional visa-free countries are very different goals. The terrorists that the United States wages war against are not uneducated and impoverished, but rather highly educated and often incredibly wealthy. Their educational and financial positions allow for clever and innovative new challenges to the United States national security. They want us to let our guard down and to focus more on making money than on security. Loosening visa control and granting more visa-free states would increase efficiency at the cost of reducing our national security.

The United States acts as an international leader and has received considerably negative ratings in recent years, but as the saying goes, "If you're not the lead sled dog, your view of the world never changes." The United States as a leader sees the changing world and adopts policies to address those changes. In this case, the United States focused its policy towards Iraq and the War on Terror. Some polling focused exclusively on these issues, often time with uninformed perspectives, rather than informing the participants of all the good policies and aid that the United States offers around the world.

Regardless of the ratings, the right policy will always be the one that offers a better future for later generations. Ranking Member Dana Rohrabacher said, "While I respect the idea that public opinion is important, what is more important is to do what is right in building a future." (Statement at the House Foreign Affairs Committee on March 22, 2007.) The United States should not determine policy based on public opinion of what policy should be, especially not public opinion of other countries, but rather choose policy based on what is right, right for the people of the United States, and will serve the international community in the long run.

www.ingramcontent.com/pod-product-compliance
Lightning Source LLC
Chambersburg PA
CBHW081758280526
45789CB00008B/2913